MW00989834

Loving Female Led Relationships

Relationships that Empower Women

Te-Erika Patterson

ACKNOWLEDGMENTS

T hank you to the awesome women and men who inspired me by sharing their stories of happy, Loving Female Led Relationships (Loving FLRs) as well as those who have come through my Loving FLR Coaching Program to share their trials and struggles so that I could help diffuse the confusion over maintaining your Loving Female Led Relationship.

I have learned so much from all of you and I am grateful to know that Loving FLRs are taking root in our society.

Te-Erika

TABLE OF CONTENTS

INTRODUCTION

G reetings and thank you for choosing to learn more about Loving Female Led Relationships (Loving FLRs). I am Te-Erika Patterson, a single Black woman, Influencer, author, relationship coach and facilitator of the FLR Matchmaking Service.

I first began studying a concept I found called Female Led Relationships in 2016. I thought it was interesting to consider that the woman could take the lead in the relationship. I initially believed that the concept of female leadership in relationships aligned with my goal to empower women in our society. Through studying the concept as a blogger, I learned that most men who were actively interested in the original FLR dynamic were guided by their desire to be controlled by a woman and to alleviate their responsibility of decision making in a relationship. I knew that I did not want to be an advocate for a relationship style that called itself Female Led yet focused more on the male's desire to be relieved from responsibility by adding more responsibility to a woman's life.

I made the shift to creating a new relationship style called **Loving** Female Led Relationships. Loving Female Led Relationships are relationships that empower women. A Loving FLR balances the destruction of our patriarchal society and allows women to finally be seen and heard so that they can contribute more to the advancement of our society. A Loving FLR actively upholds the principle that the woman's voice, opinions and desires are equally as important as any man's.

To better explain my new position, I created the LovingFLR.Com blog and I invited my audience to come with me on a new journey to empower women through loving relationships. Women in Loving FLRs are free to express their opinions and desires without their choices being viewed as secondary to the man's desires. In a Loving Female Led Relationship both individuals support and influence each other.

As a journalist, Relationship Coach, author and blogger who has coached, interviewed, surveyed and reviewed personal essays from hundreds of women and men about their relationships, it is my pleasure to introduce Loving Female Led Relationships; relationships that truly empower women.

This book is the introduction to a relationship style that will balance out the sordid impact of our patriarchal society by encouraging men to live out their soul's true desire to devote themselves to the women they love.

To join our community of highly intelligent women and men who enjoy empowering women through loving relationships please subscribe to **LovingFLR.Com**.

Te-Erika

CHAPTER 1

Does She Really Need a Man?

She doesn't believe she *needs* a man to have a good life and the truth is, she doesn't. She is independent, wise and highly skilled. She is witty, charming and sometimes brilliant. She is capable of achieving the greatness within and she knows it. She doesn't *need* a man, yet, when the right man arrives, every desire of her heart will come true much *easier* and much *faster*.

Strong women need support too. She is busy leading, providing solutions for others and being everyone's backbone and it is sad when she recognizes that she has no one there to replenish her so that she can continue to give to others. She needs someone to pour into her. She needs to be able to relax and be cared for too. Most people come to her for inspiration, solutions and validations and when she is empty, they become angry that they cannot receive the gift of her love. But who is pouring love into her so that she can continue to give love? No one. She creates self-care routines and restores herself so that she can continue to do the work that others need. Does she really need a man?

A woman who believes she doesn't need a man has yet to meet a real man. She has bided her time, wading through flakes and phonies who need her support or they feel lost in the world. When a good man arrives in a woman's life, suddenly she is able to release a weight that she had no idea she was carrying. He recognizes her strength and chooses to enhance it. He lightens her load because he is capable of doing so. *He wants to*. He is an enabler.

He stands beside her, supporting her vision because he gains pleasure from watching her shine in life. When she shines, he feels powerful knowing that he is the one holding her up to the light. He is a good man. He is a Gentleman. He is a man who will offer her the missing key she has no idea will unlock her wildest dreams. He will offer her a Loving Female Led Relationship (Loving FLR), a relationship that empowers women.

A Loving Female Led Relationship is a relationship that empowers women. All women are capable of experiencing their life dreams on their own, yet having a supportive partner to share those dreams with becomes more than a romantic fantasy, it becomes an asset.

A Loving FLR isn't dependent upon a woman's ability to control a man or aggressively demand that he support her. A Loving FLR is based on a man's desire to be the hero in a woman's life. He wants to ensure that she feels safe, secure and cared for. He wants to see her win because he believes he is a winner and he wants an equal partner by his side. A man who chooses to offer a woman a Loving FLR is offering her the peace of mind she needs to feel safe with him. When a woman feels safe, secure and cared for, she will release the hidden parts of herself. Her natural instinct to nurture and express loving devotion without restraint will be liberated and he will reap the benefit of the purest expression of her love.

Aren't Men Supposed to be the Leaders?

In our antiquated patriarchal society women and men were taught that the man is automatically the leader, that his vision should be strictly adhered to and that she should be his helpmate and submit to him. Women were taught that they shouldn't speak freely, make a fuss or even stand up for what they believed in. Women were falsely led to believe that men are more capable than they are of making the best decisions by birthright. None of these beliefs are true.

The truth is, aside from physical characteristics, every person is merely human. Our society conditions us to believe that those born with male genitalia should play out a certain role in society and those born with female genitalia should play the opposite role. That type of brainwashing restricts the growth of humanity because it limits the woman's contributions to society.

People are people and should be respected as humans. We should not be forced to act out gender roles created by ancient men attempting to prescribe the perfect path in life. As humans we all yearn for the same expressions of emotional satisfaction - affection, attention and acceptance for who we are. No one yearns to fulfill a fantasy they did not create for themselves.

Men are not automatic leaders and neither are women. The truth is, leadership should be situational. The person who wants to take the lead, has the knowledge to take the lead and has proven to be protective of the best interests of all involved should step up to lead. The leadership position should not be determined by gender, but by ability to navigate the unexpected without breaking down.

Whomever demonstrates the ability to lead should lead. Men should not be expected to lead in situations where they lack the ability to do so. We hurt men by forcing them into roles they are unprepared for or did not ask for.

In a Loving FLR, leadership is not mandated to the woman. In a Loving FLR, the man has chosen to empower the woman to express her opinions and desires without feeling stifled. When a woman feels supported in a relationship, she is free to contribute the best ideas and expressions of love that she has been taught to suppress.

This relationship style is called Loving Female LED Relationship because the man intentionally places the woman's happiness and satisfaction as the priority in the relationship. He does this because he wants to. A Loving Female Led Relationship is LED by the woman's satisfaction. The Gentleman in a Loving FLR recognizes that an emotionally supported and satisfied woman will be free to offer the absolute best of herself to him, to their family and to our society.

A man in a Loving FLR takes the time to learn exactly how the woman wants to be loved so that he can offer that to her in the way that satisfies her. He wants to be the man who satisfies her so that she has no reason to seek satisfaction elsewhere. A wise man is not foolish enough to expect a woman to offer him the type of love that he is not intentionally pouring into her. He is wise enough to understand that loving her properly according to her emotional needs is the only way to grant her the freedom to love him back in a way that satisfies him.

What Problems Does a Loving FLR Resolve?

In a typical relationship supported by patriarchal ideals, the woman has been taught to defer her opinions, goals and values for the sake of the man's preferences. She follows suit yet internally she suffers emotionally, feels neglected and grows to resent him. She can't fully love and respect a man who doesn't take the time to learn who she is or acknowledge her desires. She begins to feel trapped and dissatisfied, unconsciously sabotaging the progress of the relationship because she believes she does not matter. A Loving FLR is the remedy to common relationship issues that tear couples apart.

Lack of Confidence in the Relationship

A Loving FLR by definition empowers the woman. In practice this relationship style offers the woman the blessed opportunity to be heard by her partner. He wants to know how to please her and what she needs to feel safe, secure and cared for. When she is able to freely speak up about what she needs to feel emotionally secure with him, she learns that her voice is valid and she gains the confidence to speak up more often. When she sees that he respects her voice and opinions, she automatically develops more respect for herself.

She understands that he recognizes her worth and as a result she believes that he is the man that she deserves. When she is supported by her partner, she learns to stand up for herself in all situations because she has been taught that her voice matters. She doesn't hesitate to go after her dreams because her partner has shown her that her relationship dreams can be realized. When he makes her relationship dreams come true, she has confidence that the rest of her dreams will also come true- with him by her side.

Competitive Conflicts

When the man places the woman's satisfaction as his priority in the relationship, the woman feels safe and protected by him. She becomes less defensive in her interactions with him because she does not feel the need to compete with him so that her voice will be heard. When she knows that he is actively listening to what she wants and how she feels, she does not become easily irritated with him if he does not meet her needs exactly. She knows that he is doing his best to support her in every way that he can and she is patient and supportive of his effort.

The man in a Loving FLR benefits greatly because when she feels safe with him and conflict is reduced which leaves more space for love making and fun times. Because he wants her to win in life, he allows her to win at home, given she is not asking for anything that violates his moral stance. He will never automatically disregard her opinions and desires for the sake of his own because he enjoys knowing that when she wins, he wins.

Secret Competition

Many relationships fumble when each individual is secretly committed to the preservation of their own well-being. They both feel the need to protect themselves, even from each other because neither of them feels completely safe, secure and cared for. They do not feel as though they are truly a team so they compete with each other, reveling in the need to win against the person who is supposed to be their life partner. This is the perfect path to demise of the relationship.

In a Loving FLR there is no competition. He is devoted to ensuring that she wins and she in turn, shows appreciation for his support, ensuring that when she does win, her desires will satisfy him too.

Lack of Intimacy

In typical patriarchal relationships the woman must learn to defer her desires to his. Because she feels that she cannot speak up for herself, she withholds the information he needs to satisfy her. This ultimately leads to her resenting him for not being able to read her mind and give her what she needs without telling him. In a Loving FLR it is easy for the couple to share secret desires, honest opinions and transparent feedback because both have the same goal of ensuring that the relationship prospers. She gives him the exact instructions for how to keep her satisfied and he chooses to listen.

When couples are not truly teammates, they do not have the freedom to share the secrets of their hearts. They withhold their desires and opinions for the sake of perceived peace which ultimately drive a wedge between them because they do not believe they have a sincere love when they cannot truly express themselves.

A Loving FLR promotes intimacy between couples because he is constantly seeking to learn more about who she is and what he can do to satisfy her inner needs. When he asks questions, listens to her responses and takes note of the ways he is able to make her smile, she feels seen and heard. She opens up to him more, revealing her true self. As he meets her needs and becomes her Hero, she reciprocates by striving to protect and cherish this unique expression of love. She then encourages him to share more of who he is because she wants him to feel as safe and secure as she does.

Lack of True Commitment

When a couple does not have streamlined priorities in their relationship, they often create separate priorities which leads them down different paths that divide them. A couple who has created a Loving FLR has decided that her satisfaction is the priority in the relationship and they work together to achieve their focused intention.

When two driven individuals come together to form a team they work together toward their expressed priority. All distractions from that priority become easily dismissed. Having faith in their commitment to their Loving FLR supersedes the lack of faith that typically stems from trusting in another infallible human

Removes Pretenses

When a couple are lucky enough to form a Loving FLR they have already decided to go against social norms which relieves them of the pressure of relationship pretenses. The open minded and open-hearted couple who form a Loving FLR are now free to experiment, express and experience the type of relationship that truly satisfies them.

There are no set gender role expectations in a Loving FLR. She could be the bread winner in the family while he takes on the duty of nurturing their children. She could express that being a stay-at-home mom satisfies her soul and she wants to support his business success. He does not have to pretend to be a stereotypical stoic male who never expresses emotions. He never has to convince the woman he loves that he is a real man by holding back the expression of his feelings for her.

A couple in a Loving FLR are free to create the lifestyle they want together, without building a relationship that pleases society because they strive to satisfy each other.

CHAPTER 2

The Woman's Role in a Loving FLR

A woman involved in a Loving Female Led Relationship will feel as though she is the luckiest woman in the world. Not only does she feel respected, heard and cared for, she has found a man who is completely devoted to ensuring that she is supported in every way which, unfortunately, is not the typical relationship experience.

But how does a woman get to experience the security and bliss of a Loving Female Led Relationship? This relationship style isn't reserved for the magical women; any woman can have one if she can demonstrate that she is ready for it.

Get Ready for a Loving FLR by...

- Believe that you can have it
- Become an intentional leader
- Prepare for what you want
- Release the pain from your past
- Speak up about what bothers you
- Show appreciation for what makes you happy
- Create a life that you love right now

Believe That You Can Have It

When you are a woman who is used to building your dreams alone it can be quite difficult to believe that a man is capable of coming into your life to support what you have built. You're probably thinking - *If a man couldn't support you before then why the hell would you need one now?*

You may be a woman who has yet to build your dreams because life has beat you down so many times that you are not sure that you can ever achieve the goals dancing around in your brain. You may have spent so many years giving yourself over to support the men who came into and out of your life that you feel as though you have no energy left for yourself and you are tired, oh so tired. When you do not believe you can have the type of relationship that you want, you will reject it when it does appear.

No matter where you are right now, there is a man who can and will support you. The most important thing stopping you from having this experience is your belief that you cannot have it. When you believe that good men do not exist, you push away the experience.

How I (Almost) Pushed Away a Good Man

My last relationship was nearly 20 years ago. That relationship impacted my ability to allow love in and I vowed to never allow another man to get close to me or to give my love to anyone ever again. Over the years men would try to love me but I automatically assumed it was the precursor to an attack.

I believed that men who offered their love to me were only doing so because they secretly wanted to hurt me intentionally. This wasn't a conscious belief, it became deeply imbedded in my psyche so I would lash out in anger at any man who stayed around too long, hoping to push him away before he could try to hurt me. This worked very well and each time I was successful at pushing a man away, I felt safe again.

When I met it him was a random day at a Second Line parade in New Orleans and I was hot, sweaty and happy to be out and about in my favorite city. He marched next to me, I said Hi and he made me laugh within a minute. We spent the rest of the evening together and it felt…comfortable. I am used to sweet beginnings and ours was very sweet. He was great at catering to me, being there for me and genuinely making me feel like I was living in a fairytale. I couldn't believe I had found a man that I enjoyed being with so much and I wanted a future with.

A month after we met *something* happened. I blamed him. He blamed me. Whoever was to blame, everything changed and we turned into monsters towards each other. At this point you would think that we would walk away but neither of us did. We spent months tearing each other down with me accusing him of trying to hurt me, demanding that he do things my way and returning my aggression with his own, more venomous version.

We spent the next year and a half fighting every single time we spoke. We broke up, got back together and broke up again. I would feel relieved when we broke up because then I would feel safe again. I knew that because of my past trauma I was expressing my anger towards him and he was returning it. In essence, I was leading the relationship towards turmoil by the way I was treating him. Exactly what did I do to cause turmoil in my relationship?

- I imagined the worst behaviors and accused him of them
- I analyzed every word he said, trying to catch him in a lie
- I berated him often for not meeting my expectations
- I made sure to always tell him how disappointed I was with him
- I compared him to other men who I felt were better than he was
- I encouraged him to be with other women who were more on his level
- I ignored him when he asked me to please be his peace
- I blamed him for every problem we had
- I was uncompromising and selfish; he had to do it my way or he didn't love me

Be an Intentional Leader

I was leading us towards turmoil with my aggression towards him. Was I doing it on purpose? No. I had no idea that I was sabotaging my chances at love by being defensive and aggressive. I thought I was protecting myself. Once I recognized that this was happening, after nearly 2 years, I changed my behavior and began to interact with him in a way that was intentional and focused more on the behavior I wanted him to mirror back to me.

An intentional leader is someone who deliberately uses words and actions that will elicit the behavior or reaction they want from the person they are engaging with. The intentional leader understands how their words and actions will impact the person they are engaging with and uses this knowledge to steer their exchanges towards the results they want.

I began to intentionally offer him compliments and praise. I intentionally stepped back, demanded less and became more understanding and accepting of who he was as a man. I intentionally showed more respect for his opinions. I intentionally led us back to being kind to each other. At this point I realized that I finally had what I wanted, a Loving Female Led Relationship.

Prepare for What You Want

If you want a good relationship like a Loving FLR you should prepare for it. How can you best prepare for a

Loving FLR? Focus more on what you want instead of what you do not want.

It may make you feel as though you are being resourceful when you make preparations to ward off harm, yet, all of that energy that you spend meditating on the worst possible outcomes could be better spent preparing for the good life that awaits you.

Do you want to vacation more? Get a second job or start a new business. Do you want a partner who is fit? Create your own fitness routine and stick with it so that you can match with your fantasy partner? Do you imagine yourself being a highly celebrated leader in our society? Go out and create a social service that benefits your own community. Do you want a loving partner? Show love and kindness to the people you meet on a daily basis. Prepare more for what you want instead of bracing for what you do not want.

Release the Pain from Your Past

Even though people may have hurt you in the past, it doesn't mean that it is a curse that will follow you into your future. If you want a new ending you must choose a new beginning. Your new beginning starts when you decide it does. Draw a line in the sand. Determine that when you cross the line, your luck changes with it.

Practice your new luck by keeping your eye out for a dime on the ground. The next time you find a dime on the ground pick it up and place it in your palm. The energy from this sign from the Universe is your new beginning.

The troubles that took place in your past had no bearings on your future. The people who may have hurt you were battling their own pain and had no choice but to release it onto the next person they met, which happened to be you. Their hurtful behavior has nothing to do with who you are and what you deserve from life. You deserve a good life. You deserve a good partner. You deserve to be cared for, to feel supported and secure. You can have it and you will have it when you accept that it is possible.

Speak Up About What Bothers You

As you prepare for your Loving FLR it is important to practice for the new life you will live by speaking up when something bothers you. People only respect the boundaries they know about. If you do not tell people when they have offended you or given you less than what you want, they will not know to correct it. I know that you have been taught to keep quiet in order to keep the peace. They say good girls don't make waves but you have to realize that you are not a girl anymore. You are a grown woman. You were meant to take up space. Your life matters. Your opinions matter. Your voice matters.

Practice speaking up today by correcting anyone who does or says something that offends you. You don't have to correct them aggressively. You can simply say, "Please be mindful when you speak to me. I don't like what you just said." Be firm but polite. You will get your point across and the person will respect you more.

Show Appreciation for What Makes You Happy

Life is not set up to cater to all of your whims. When someone does something that makes you happy it is important to acknowledge it for yourself and for them. When you acknowledge someone's good behavior the words you speak replays in their minds and they subconsciously seek to hear those words again because it gives them an energy boost. This motivates them to repeat the behavior so that they can experience the emotional reward.

When you get into the habit of expressing appreciation for the good deeds of others, you extend some of that appreciation energy to yourself. So often we gloss over the good times and meditate on the bad times because the excitement of the stress of the negative moments is somehow rewarding us emotionally. We can shift that. Instead of meditating on the negative moments to experience your emotional reward, relish in the good moments when you were delivered exactly what you wanted or better.

I sometimes catch myself in bed smiling thinking about how far I have come in life. I am truly living out the best times in my life that I have ever had. It is amazing to be still and think about how I never imagined the tough times would lead me here.

It feels very silly when you catch yourself being appreciative of the good in your life, yet the silliness is warm and comforting. It feels like when you were a kid waiting to wear your new outfit on the first day of school. That joyful anticipation will repeat itself when you learn to openly acknowledge the good times you experience in life and with others. Appreciating and acknowledging the good in your life also energizes YOU because you began to recognize just how much you have to be grateful for.

Create a Life that You Love Right Now

If you would love to experience the joy of having a man to support your goals and desires in life, it would be best to create a life that you actually enjoy. When he meets you, he will appreciate what you have done with your life and want to be a part of it. A good man may not want to rescue you or build you up from scratch. If you are looking for a rescuer to carry the weight of your desires, this relationship style isn't for you.

A good man, a man who yearns for a Loving FLR, wants to be an asset to a woman's life, he doesn't want to be her savior. Get started on your dreams and goals right now and build yourself up. When you meet him his support will take you the rest of the way.

Be His Safe Space

The key ingredient to creating a Loving Female Led Relationship is not the woman's ability to lead or express her desires. The key ingredient to creating a Loving FLR is the man's decision to be a willing supporter of her happiness. Without his active devotion she cannot have a Loving FLR.

Many women believe the key to getting a man to support them is to demand that he does. Demanding support from men only works with men who were abused by their mothers and female family members. If you are able to snag a man by being aggressive, controlling or demanding, he may be in love with you now, but what will happen if one day you are sick or unable to express the aggression? Without exerting forcefulness, will he still be attracted to you or will he seek the aggression and abuse he needs from someone else?

 A Gentleman wants to give you the desires of your heart and he does not need for you to demand it. He wants to support you freely because he enjoys it. If you feel that you have to nag or demand his love and support, it is likely that he does not love you or he does not feel safe with you. The best way to encourage him to love you freely is to create a relationship where he feels safe with you emotionally and intimately.

You can ensure that a man feels safe with you by:

- Allowing him the time to learn how to love you
- Expressing your vision your best relationship
- Listening to his needs and providing those you are able to
- Accepting him as he is
- Correcting him with kindness (privately)
- Affirming him
- Creating an environment that he wants to come to for replenishment
- Trust him to be his best and offer his best
- Elevating his ego

Allow Him Time to Learn How to Love You

Unless your partner was raised in the same home with the same parents as you were he won't know you so intimately that he can satisfy you when you first meet him. He won't know how to love you at first and you will need to be patient enough to allow him to get to know you. No one will ever play out your fantasy relationship exactly how you imagine because we do not live in a fantasy world. Life is not a movie. In this world people have the freedom to choose who they interact with. If a man is choosing to interact with you, he is choosing to try to learn how to engage with you peacefully and he won't get it right immediately.

He can't read your mind. He didn't see that one movie you saw where the man was perfect. He will try to ensure that you feel loved but it will take time for him to get it right. Please be patient with him. Take the time to speak up and correct him kindly when he is not loving you properly because- he doesn't know how to do it yet. He will never know how to love you unless you tell him. He can't guess. He isn't psychic. He needs you to tell him and show him by example. Be patient with him. If he puts in effort to show you love in the way you want it, he is a good man. You do not have to rush the process; he will get there.

Paint a Vision for Your Best Relationship

If you want a good man to support your vision for your relationship you must express your vision consistently so that he can agree and create ways to support it. He will feel safe with you when he understands that you plan to have him as a permanent part of your life and you are sure that your life together will be wonderful.

Express your vision with your words. Share positive predictions with stories about your future together that include the best-case scenarios that you can imagine. When you share a vision of your life together and he can visualize it, he will believe that he can create that wonderful life with you and he will do everything he can to support your vision.

Listen to His Needs

A man who desires to support you in every way that he can is a good man and he should never be taken for granted. Although he is skilled and eager to please you, his needs, opinions and desires are important too. He will share them with you if he feels safe with you. Please do not ignore him or brush his needs aside in favor of your own. His simple requests should be honored. When you allow a man to feel important by meeting his needs, he will likely go to the ends of the earth to meet yours.

Allow him to vent, to share stories and to express his opinions even when you disagree with him. Men want to feel heard which validates their existence. In a world where men must fight to be recognized amongst other men, he will know for a fact that you are the one person who truly sees him and values him.

Accept Him as He Is

When a man feels safe with you, he will reveal things about himself that very few other people will ever know. Some of the secrets he will share may seem weird but the more weird the secret is, the more honored you should feel that he has shared it with you. He feels safe enough to be his weirdest self and that is a reflection of how well you love him. As long as his interests or preferences are not physically or emotionally debilitating, indulge him.

Become the one person on earth that he can shed his inhibitions with. If you can accept him for who he really is, it is very likely that he will not stray because he will understand that no one else will love him for his real self in the way that you do.

Offer Affirmative Correction

If he has bad habits that you believe are hurting his chances at living a long and fulfilling life then it is important to correct him directly. Outside of bad habits that may be hurting his health or sabotaging the long-term success of your family, if he does things that annoy you, you should correct him, but please do it with kindness instead of aggression.

Eating in bed is not a cause for a fist fight. Shaving his toe nails in the living room is not a cause for a melt-down. Leaving his chewed gum on the edges of dinner plates is not a reason to yell at him. All of these bad habits are signs that he is alive and living with you. If he were to die, all of these signs of life would be missing and you would miss them.

To determine if his bad habits are worth aggressive correction ask yourself – If he died and you went to his funeral, while looking at his dead body in the casket would you be able to say, "I'm so glad he's dead because now I don't have to deal with (insert annoying habit)."

If you would **not** be grateful that he's dead because you no longer have to deal with the bad habit then it does not deserve aggressive correction.

When you must correct him, please wait until you are in private to do so. Correcting him publicly or shaming him for not meeting your expectations will only undermine the safety and trust he has in your relationship. When you make statements that make him feel stupid, he will begin to act stupidly. Your aggressive criticism of his flaws is a sure way to sabotage his support of your relationship.

Instead of aggressively correcting him for tasks that he has not made a habit of completing properly, you can offer him affirmative correction by thanking him for doing the things that he has forgotten or ignored even if he has yet to do them.

Examples of Affirmative Correction

- Thank you for remembering to wash the cars this weekend.
- Thank you for reminding me when the insurance is due.
- Thank you for being so understanding when I have to work late.
- Thank you for taking out the garbage.
- Thank you for the birthday gift.
- Thank you for being patient with me when I couldn't find the correct address.

Offering affirmative correction lets him know that you recognize his mistake and you have faith that his ass will get it right one of these days.

Affirm Him

Every man putting effort into pleasing the woman he loves wants to know when he is doing a good job. You don't have to throw a party every time he remembers to take out the garbage but speaking words of affirmation to him gives him a standard to try to live up to.

If you want a good man, call him a good man. If you want a faithful partner, tell him you are glad that he is such a faithful partner. If you want a hero, call him your hero. He will remember the words that you have spoken to him and subconsciously try to live up to them.

Create a Replenishing Environment

If you have a good man who wants to give you the world then he is likely putting in a lot of effort, sweat and time to make your dreams come true. Wouldn't it be a good reward to create an environment where he looks forward to coming to for replenishment?

Give him a clean and cozy home to come back to. Greet him with a kiss and a smile when you see him no matter how your day went. Dress up for him. Whisper words of comfort and appreciation to him after he has had a long day. Offer him his favorite treats both inside and outside of the bedroom. Say Yes to him often when he asks for little things. Offer him the water he needs both literally and figuratively so that you will become the source of the replenishment that he cannot find anywhere else.

Trust Him to Offer His Best

It is easy to trust a man when he is doing things you want him to do but to truly help a man to feel safe with you must demonstrate that you trust him even when he is not. If you believe that you are a capable and smart woman who makes great decisions for her life then you have to believe that you are capable of choosing a man who honors you and also makes great decisions for his life.

When you choose a man who wants to offer you a Loving FLR, or even if you are creating one without his knowledge by following this chapter's advice, you should understand that allowing a man the freedom to express his best effort without micro managing him or belittling his attempt is the best way to demonstrate love.

You may think your fantasies of what love should look like are the only way to experience a love that satisfies you but sometimes the love he gives on his own can blow any fantasy you may have out of the water. Trust that his plans, intentions and actions will please you and give him space for creative expression of his love.

Even on those days when your faith in him is diminishing, trust that you made a good decision by choosing him and demonstrate it by giving him more space to grow.

Elevate His Ego

When you realize that you have a good man who is giving you a Loving FLR, it is best to make it a point to elevate his ego. Point out the great traits you see in him when you are talking to him and especially when you are speaking about him to others. You should not have to lie and brag about things that are not true. Your purpose is to identify the ways he has added stability, love and progress to your life and praise him for doing it to his face and behind his back.

A man's ego is fragile and will be shattered at the mere mention that he has not done something to your satisfaction. When you shatter his ego it reduces his strength mentally and physically and he will become too mentally weak to provide the support and encouragement you need to maintain your family's peace.

Elevating his ego ensures that he knows that you recognize his value. When a man believes that you recognize his value he strives to become more valuable to you, your family and to the world.

Remind him that he is your lucky charm and treat him as such. No matter what drama is happening in your life or how sad the latest world news report makes you feel, remember that he is the one person who has chosen to stand with you in this lifetime. The type of devotion he is offering isn't his obligation. He is choosing to give it to you. You are a lucky woman to have him and you should make every effort to let him know that you are grateful for him.

5 Truths About Leading a Loving FLR

You have to know what you want.

Your partner in a Loving FLR cannot support your vision and success if you do not know what you want from your relationship or your life. You will have to be direct and tell him how to support you and to do this you must know what you want from him and express it directly.

He can't guess what you want or read in between the lines to figure it out. When you are following a map you do not want to have to decode the directions, you want everything to be clear so that you can reach your destination efficiently.

How do you determine what you want? Creating your vision for your relationship is not just about having him cater to you and pamper you. What is your idea of a good relationship? Which types of experiences do you want you and your partner to share? What can your partner do to ensure that you feel safe, secure and cared for? Share the answers to these questions with your partner to jumpstart your Loving FLR.

Your relationship's success is your responsibility.

Every good leader is a good servant of those she leads. This means that although you may have a partner who is devoted to your success and prosperity you must fuel his devotion by taking excellent care of his needs so that he has the energy to continue to support you.

When you notice that he is unhappy, unmotivated or irritated instead of asking, What's wrong with him? Ask yourself, *What can I do to improve his mood?*

It is the woman's responsibility to set the vision for the relationship and to do everything in her power to support her own vision including making sure to support her partner in ways that he cannot get from any other woman.

Lead with your energy.

When you determine the vision for your relationship be sure that it includes the feeling or energy you want to experience. You may decide that you want to experience a peaceful energy or a joyful energy, but, whichever energy you decide that you want you must be willing to give that same energy to your partner consistently.

Amplify your partner's strengths and make up for his weaknesses.

Crafting the ideal Loving FLR isn't about passing off the household chores you do not want to do to your partner because he is intent to support you. A good leader recognizes the strengths and weaknesses of her partner and delegates tasks that he is more proficient at so that he will be successful in his support.

You would never ask a toddler to be your driver just because you do not like to drive. You give the responsibility of certain tasks to the person who is most capable of achieving them efficiently.

Make firm decisions and be confident in them.

You do not have to take the lead in all decisions because you are in a partnership and not a dictatorship. You take the lead in decisions that are best suited for your knowledge and skills and delegate other decisions to your partner that are better suited for him. When you do have a decision to make, be confident in it. There is no decision that you can make that will permanently destroy you. Make decisions that are in the best interest of your RELATIONSHIP, not yourself. Make decisions with the best intentions for both of you and let the chips fall where they may.

CHAPTER 3

The Man's Benefit in a Loving FLR

The man who engages in a Loving FLR is truly the definition of a Gentleman. A Gentleman is always gentle with women. As a Gentleman, he vows to secure the heart of the woman he adores. He wants to be the source of her happiness. He wants to be the instrument that provides joy, peace and prosperity for her. He believes that his most blissful, peaceful and fulfilling place in life, is in the arms of the woman who loves him. He wants to be her hero. Her happiness is his greatest pride.

He is a man who desires to release the secret part of himself that yearns to shower her with affection, attention and pleasure. He is not a man who needs to be pleased; his pleasure lies in pleasing her. He believes his manhood is a reflection of how well he cares for the woman he loves. A Loving Female Led Relationship allows him the freedom to live out his true purpose.

Freedom from Aggression

A man who engages in a Loving FLR frees himself from the confines of male aggressive behavior towards women. Men do not naturally desire to dominate and overpower women; men want to serve and support women. Men are usually aggressive with women when they fear the woman does not respect them. These men believe expressing aggression towards a woman will create the respect they have been denied, yet it really demonstrates his feeling of powerlessness.

A man who engages in a Loving FLR no longer has to prove his manliness by being aggressive towards a woman. He knows he is respected and appreciated by the woman he loves and he can be his true self, the man who only wants to support her happiness.

Understanding His Power

A man in a Loving FLR does not feel powerless, in fact he understands just how powerful he is. Just like a man cannot create a baby without a woman, a woman cannot create a Loving FLR without the consistent support of a man. A Loving FLR is a gift that he chooses to give to her. Although he enjoys saying Yes to her requests, he is not obligated to do so. If she asks him to do anything that violates his core values, he has every right to say No and she must respect it.

When he engages with a Powerful Woman and manages to empower her to achieve a richer version of happiness and success, he understands that his power is unlimited. The majority of the world's population is sad, angry and depressed because they have not experienced the empowerment of being loved properly. A man in a Loving FLR gives this type of empowerment to the woman of his choice and the world is a better place because of his choice.

Keeps Him Focused on a Specific Goal

Smart men enjoy achieving goals and seeing measurable results. A Loving FLR is his own personal mission to ensure the happiness of the woman he loves and he measures it by her satisfaction which he can experience daily. A Loving FLR gives him a solid goal to work toward. If she is smiling and achieving her dreams, happy to come home to him and expressing her greatness in the world, then he knows he is doing his job as a Gentleman in a Loving FLR. Her happiness is his success.

Inner Peace

Most extraordinary men do not wish to fight the inner battle associated with upholding preconceived notions about who they are and how they should interact with the world. Many of men's aggressive tendencies toward women stem from wanting to be themselves completely and give themselves over to the service of the woman they love. They fear that they will be seen as weak if they say Yes too much or become too accommodating so they say No out of fear even when their hearts want to say Yes.

Men in Loving FLRs do not have this fear. They are able to release the hidden parts of themselves because they understand that the nurturing trait the world pushes them to hide is the very trait that their wives find endearing.

He exposes his true supportive nature to her and she falls deeper in love with him because as a Powerful Woman she has no desire for a partner to overtake her. She wants a partner to help accommodate her biggest dreams. He does not have to shrink himself or play a role for this society any longer. He is truly able to be at peace with himself.

True Expression of His Love

Men are attracted to women for obvious reasons and one of them is the softness they carry with them. Men have the same softness within their character and they admire that women are free to express this tenderness without shame. Men in Loving FLRs can openly express their feelings of love without feeling stifled or ashamed. The Loving FLR itself is an open expression of devoted love that most men cannot attain.

Provides Direction

The Loving FLR provides direction to the relationship because his quest is to understand who she is and what he can do to ensure that she feels safe, secure and cared for. Listening to her express herself, respecting what she says and how she feels is paramount for a man in a Loving FLR.

Understanding his partner's love languages and nuances to better give her the love she needs is a symbol of a powerful man. He has clear instructions for how to please her and unlike most men he uses these instructions like a map to guarantee their happy life together.

He Plays the Role He Really Wants

Many may not realize that most people do not want to take the lead in life situations. Most people are not natural leaders and this particular role is forced upon men in our society whether they want to play it or not. In a Loving FLR a man is not required to make all of the decisions alone and bear the weight of holding the family together by himself.

The woman in a Loving FLR does not make all of the decisions alone because she is not a dictator. She offers input for her vision for their relationship and he supports her vision. He enjoys supporting her vision. He prefers to allow her to create the details for how they can create their happy life together and he demonstrates his strength by laying the foundation. He is so smart that he is capable of carrying out her wishes, both big and small and it truly pleases him to do so.

Stress at Work, Peace at Home

A man in a Loving FLR is most often a man who is driven professionally. When he is driven professionally, he is under a lot of pressure to achieve which adds a surmountable amount of stress to his life. Luckily, the Loving FLR allows him to leave the stress at work and he is able to enjoy peace at home. At work, the progress of his labor depends on so many external factors and contributions from a wide variety of people. His home life has an established priority of supporting one woman's vision with clear instructions for how to do so. He can relax and follow her lead.

The Power to Satisfy His Partner

There are stories of men who go to great lengths to escape their wives simply because they do not know how to satisfy them. The Gentleman in a Loving FLR looks forward to going home each night because he recognizes that he possesses the knowledge to make sure his wife is happy.

What a great gift to give to someone, the desire and power to make them smile every day. When he takes the time to learn what his partner likes and actually makes effort to do it, he sees immediate results that let him know that he is doing well. Because there are no guessing games he has a clear path to satisfy her.

He Can Create a Boss

When a man wants a woman to boss up, the best thing he can do to motivate her is to treat her like a boss. A man in a Loving FLR empowers a woman to go out into the world and take charge when he allows her the freedom to take charge at home.

Understanding His Role in a Loving FLR

A man's engagement in a Loving FLR does not relinquish him of responsibilities. He now has the added responsibility of supporting another person's happiness which is far more difficult than honoring his own self-serving needs.

Happy Wife, Happy Life – and don't forget it. But how can he ensure his wife is happy?

When she wants something specific, he offers it to her without hesitation. He doesn't feel that her desires are too much for him to deliver and he knows she is worth the effort. When you allow a woman to have her way, and she's not a selfish woman, she will soften to the point where having her way isn't as important anymore and she will then make decisions that benefit the relationship instead of herself.

For example, if you starve a monkey and finally give it a banana it will ravish the banana, leaving none to share with its partner. When the monkey has had enough to eat and knows it can have more anytime it wants, when offered a banana it will take a small bite and share with its partner.

When a man consistently denies a woman's needs, when she finally gets her way, she takes full control and does not consider his needs. When a man consistently cares for a woman's needs, she becomes full and satisfied and will think clearly enough to want to offer the same to her loving partner

Every man is capable of being a good man in a Loving FLR, yet most men are not aware that they have the option to do so. When a man has not experienced successes in life, he feels as though he has to compete with every person he meets in order to validate himself. This competition spills over into his relationships with women. He has to compete with the women he loves and win, or else his mind will give into the nagging belief that he is a loser.

A good man in a Loving FLR does not need to dominate a woman because he has nothing to prove to the world, to her or himself. He knows that he is a winner and supporting her so that she wins makes him feel like a genie in a bottle.

How to Drive a Woman Away

In our current society women are more empowered to be self-sufficient than ever before. Being a wife is no longer necessary and marriage is an option. A man who secures the love of a woman must work to maintain that love if he wants a woman to share his life with. If he commits the following offenses, a woman will have no problem walking away.

- Behaving as though caring for her is a chore
- Showing her that her needs are not important by ignoring them
- Placing his commitment to his work above his commitment to her
- Spending the majority of his time with friends while ignoring her
- Allowing strangers to treat her with more reverence and respect
- Focusing only on his sexual satisfaction
- Making decisions that impact her without asking for her input
- Yelling at her or becoming aggressive
- Openly engaging in habits that will hurt his health

How to Create Peace in a Loving FLR

If either of you are feeling negative, irritated or angry about a situation that happened outside of the relationship, learn to protect the energy of your partner by not interacting with them until you release that chaotic energy. When you pass along that chaotic energy to your partner, neither of you can sleep well, enjoy each other or move forward with your goals together.

Protect Each Other's Energy

Take a moment to sit in the car, go for a run or take a long shower when you are filled with angst from a stressful situation. Calm your energy before engaging with your partner. Your partner deserves all of the peace you can offer them because the world is already offering enough angst and you are supposed to be their refuge.

Neutralize the Situation

A man's greatest strength in any committed relationship is to be able to calm a woman's heart. He can calm a woman's heart by learning how to neutralize an emotional situation that has gotten out of hand.

If the situation was caused by a miscommunication with him, he should always apologize first. He should say the actual words- *I am sorry.*

Apologizing first lets the woman know that he takes responsibility, not for the incident, but for whatever miscommunication happened that upset her spirit. When he apologizes first, she feels that her emotional pain has been acknowledged. Acknowledgement of her emotional distress is the first step she needs towards releasing it.

How to Satisfy a Woman

The Gentleman recognizes that he is truly a Gentleman when he can state that he is always gentle with women. **He has the privilege of being the man to elevate her and comfort her.**

A Gentleman does not crave an assertive woman because he has no desire to place her in a situation where she has to assert herself with him.

There should never be an incident where he needs to overpower a woman or aggressively put a woman in her place. The only time a man should put a woman in her place is when he is placing her on a pedestal.

Placing a woman on a pedestal and striving to keep her there is the best way to satisfy a woman. Try these other tips for creating a satisfied partner in a Loving FLR.

Agree With Her Dreams

You do not have to fully commit to every idea or goal she has. The mere fact that she has come to you to share her hopes and dreams means that she trusts you with them. Be a source of encouragement by allowing her to share her full vision and find something you can agree with about her vision. It is important to agree with her dreams verbally so that she feels supported. A simple - *Yes, I can see how that would be a great idea* – is good enough. Find something about that dream that you can agree on and expound on that detail to give her a boost, asking her to share more.

Then find a way to be a part of making her vision come true. If you do not believe that her vision is feasible for her or beneficial for your family, then ask to have a discussion about the best way to go about it. During this discussion you can bring up the obstacles you anticipate and figure out ways to overcome them.

Never say NO to a woman's vision without offering an alternative way to help her achieve what she wants.

Examples:

SHE: I want to go to Maui in 2 weeks.

HE: Yes, we can spend a few days in Maui in 2 weeks but if we have time to do a little more saving, we might be able to spend 2 whole weeks in Maui this summer instead of a weekend. Let's choose which would be best for us.

SHE: I want to buy a new car.

HE: Yes. You definitely deserve a new car. Have you thought about which car you want? Can you send me a list of what you are looking for and I'll come up with a few options for us.

SHE: I think I should go back to school.

HE: Yes. Education is important and I support that. Let's talk about how we can adjust our family routine to make time for it.

Comfort her emotions without trying to solve the problem.

Just listen to her when she is having a bad day or needs to talk a situation through. Before you speak up, ask her- *Do you want comfort or advice?*

You never have to ask her What's wrong? Asking her *What is wrong?* will only make her relive the hurtful situation. Instead of asking her *What's wrong?* Just tell her that everything will be alright.

You don't need to know the details of the situation because the details will change with the next situation but her emotions won't. It doesn't matter what the situation is exactly, it matters that she knows you have faith that she can overcome anything. Just hug her and say- *Everything will be alright.* The next time she faces a situation that stresses her she will think of you and remember those words and she will be comforted by the memory of your comfort.

Just listen to her when she is having a bad day or needs to talk a situation through. Before you speak up, ask her- *Do you want comfort or advice?*

Make sure she FEELS loved.

You can buy a thousand roses or fly her to Hawaii but if those actions don't make her *feel* loved, you will never experience the love you truly want in return because she will not be satisfied. Hold back on doing things that *you* believe indicate love and focus on learning what makes *her* feel loved. Start doing those things instead.

When She Is Hurting

Understand that when a woman is hurting the best way to resolve the pain is to touch her, hold her and tell her everything will be okay. You cannot reason with a woman or try to convince her that her emotional pain is insignificant. Doing so will only drive her away from you.

When a woman is hurting, she is filled with so much pain that she can only give out the equal amount of pain that she has inside. You cannot expect her to love you properly and be her most brilliant self when she feels neglected or misunderstood. She will lash out. She will cause you the same pain she feels inside, not because she enjoys hurting you, but because she can only give what she has inside of her. If she is filled with pain and anger, you will feel the brunt of it.

The best way to help relieve her emotional pain is to replace the pain with love, your love. Give her a reason to smile. Do something kind for her. Hug her more often. Tell her she is beautiful. Instead of running away when she lashes out, draw closer to her and hold her. You cannot change her with your aggression or by withholding love from her until she *acts right.* If you understand why she is giving out pain, the pain she offers should not hurt you. You can easily relieve the pain for both of you by pouring more love into her to replace the pain she feels. The more love you give to her, the more love she will have to give back to you.

Please Her, Protect Her, Promote Her.

Pleasing the woman you love comes with specific instructions. The prefix 'PL' of Please indicates multiple. The root word 'Ease' indicates keeping her at ease. You are required to keep her at ease in multiple ways. You can create multiple ways to keep her at ease by focusing on her pleasure and peace of mind. Ask yourself- How can I provide pleasure and peace to her day?

Protecting the woman you love is an important demonstration of your love for her. You will protect her from physical harm. You will also protect her mental health and well-being. You will protect her emotions by not being double minded and honoring your word. Keep yourself healthy and do not expose her to unhealthy habits and environments.

If she complains that others are being disruptive to her peace of mind in any way, make a plan to remove the stressors or remove her from the situation immediately. Do not allow turmoil to linger in her life. Protect her from financial devastation. You are charged with protecting her from discord and dissatisfaction.

Promoting the woman you love is your daily objective. Promote her by always speaking well of her to others, reminding her of her vision and taking action to help her achieve it. Be an advocate for your her. Take action toward her goals as though they are your own.

Offer Active Support

Support is an action word; it is not moral support or well wishes. You can't offer *thoughts and prayers* unless your thoughts and prayers can drive or pay a bill. How do you offer Active Support to the woman you love?

When she mentions any goal, desire or issue she is facing, you intentionally create a way to be a part of making the desire a reality or making the issue less stressful. You don't have to take over her project f*or her*, all you have to do is demonstrate that you heard her and you are standing with her by taking action.

- If she mentions she is thinking about becoming a homeowner, you can – *sign her up for homeowner education classes.*
- If she says she is ready to start a new business, you can – *order her first set of business cards.*
- If she is busy working on renovations for your new home, you can - *make sure to order dinner for her every night to relieve pressure.*
- If she is worried about her ill mother, you can - *offer to drive her to go visit her Mom.*
- If she is constantly working on losing weight, you can – *buy her a workout outfit and tell her that she looks like she's losing weight already.*

- If she mentions she heard of a great recipe she wants to try, you can- *surprise her with a grocery gift card to encourage her to try it.*
- If she says she is stressed out, you can – *make sure she has an orgasm.*

Verbal support is wonderful and absolutely necessary. Amazing women love to hear praise from their partners, but your **active support,** lets her know that you believe in her, that she is all powerful and she can do anything - *with you by her side.*

CHAPTER 4

How to Create a Loving FLR

A couple that creates a Loving Female Led Relationship chooses peace and prosperity for their relationship. Although every Loving FLR is different there a few common ways to ensure that your relationship has the best chance of being sustainable.

How to Recognize a Worthy Partner

What makes a Loving FLR so great? Two great people who make the choice to form a Loving FLR so that they experience the bliss of mutual satisfaction. You can recognize that you have a partner worthy of creating a sustainable Loving FLR when your interaction with them reveals these traits.

You feel safe with them.

A couple in a Loving FLR work together to ensure that they both feel safe emotionally, physically and financially. You won't expect the worst from your partner. You won't feel as though you are always on guard. Out in the world anything can happen and it is common to brace for the worst but with your partner you truly believe they would never do anything intentionally to hurt you.

You respect their judgment.

You feel safe with your partner and this safety carries over to the instances where your partner has to correct you or offer criticism. You want to hear how your partner feels about your decisions or your goals and when they offer their opinion you respect their judgment because you understand that they are there to protect you from harm.

You feel valued by them.

There is nothing that boosts your confidence more than knowing that your partner truly loves and values your presence in their life. They not only tell you how much you mean to them they show you by placing you as a priority. You never feel neglected or cast to the side for the needs of outsiders. You come first and they never hesitate to show you.

You realize that you make a good team.

A Loving FLR thrives when the couple works together as a team. He works diligently to ensure that she feels secure and cared for while she does the work of uplifting the family and keeping the peace. Duties are divided by skillset and you work hand in hand to tackle life's inconsistencies without pushing one person to shoulder all of the responsibility. You are a team and you work well together to achieve your relationship's dreams.

You seek to understand each other.

When two people come together to form a Loving FLR they understand that they will have differences of opinions, preferences and even the pace at which they handle life maintenance duties. You will also understand that your separate life experiences and family influences have impacted the way you interact with each other and the world.

Instead of judging each other for not reacting to situations identically, you seek to understand why your partner offers the reaction. You either accept it or help them to adjust it if it is damaging to the relationship.

You want to see each other win.

There is no competition in a Loving FLR. He doesn't feel as though he needs to manipulate her to get what he wants from her. She doesn't feel as though she has to hide her true intentions or he will not support her. You want to see each other win. Although he takes great care to ensure that she feels heard and her desires are met, she will often take a step back to allow him the space to feel victorious by meeting his needs and standing behind him when he has a desire or goal. When she wins, he wins and vice versa. You both work together to ensure that you both feel like winners in love and in life.

You are good for each other.

Someone who is good for you brings out the good IN you. You feel like you are at your best when your partner is by your side. You feel as though you can achieve anything with your partner in your corner. Your knowledge or skills may not match exactly yet you count it as an asset that your wisdom complements each other perfectly. You are good for each other. You make each other feel good. You see the good in each other and you believe it is a reflection of the good in you.

You feel protected.

While average couples behave as though their partner is their adversary you know that your partner is your protector. You respect your partner for uplifting you in their presence and when you are out of sight. You truly believe that your partner would never do anything to damage the peace and progress of the relationship.

You trust your partner to always give their best.

Even on those days when you feel shaky about the world, you look at your partner and you respect that they are giving their very best effort to your relationship. Trust doesn't always come easily but you work at it, sometimes biting your lip to keep the negativity in. Even when your partner does not meet your expectations precisely you can give them a pass because you understand that no one is perfect. Their consistent presence, showing up every day, choosing you every day, becomes your new definition of giving your best.

You honor each other's gifts.

When a couple forms a Loving FLR it is likely because they complement each other. Being a complement to each other often indicates that where one lacks in skill, the other takes up for it. In average relationships the couple is often at war, belittling each other's efforts and talents so that they can feel superior. In a Loving FLR, the couple comes together to help each other strengthen their talents when they can. The couple in a Loving FLR respect their professional differences and talents, striving to become the loudest cheerleader and advocates for each other.

You have each other's backs.

There is no situation that you will go alone. When your car breaks down, your partner is there. When you are in the hospital sick, your partner is there with you. If you lose your bank card, you can use your partner's. When you are having a bad day, count on your partner for a hug or a listening ear.

Your partner will never leave you to struggle alone or watch you fumble without offering their arm to steady you. Even if they do not have the knowledge to help you, they will do their best to stand in the situation with you and keep you encouraged. This type of friend, willing to rescue you from hell or sit right there with you until you both get out, is the best fit for a partner.

Identify Why You are a Good Fit Together

What is it about your relationship that makes you a good fit to create a Loving FLR? There should be many reasons yet, it is important to acknowledge them as a reminder during those times when life's inconsistencies, trials and doubts cause you to believe otherwise.

Take turns answering these questions together.

- When did I realize that I loved you?
- What do you do that leads me to believe that I can trust you?
- In which ways do we match each other?
- In which ways do our differences complement each other?
- How do I know that I am a priority in your life?
- How would my life be worse if you were not a part of it?

How did this exercise make you feel? Did you come to realize that you truly are a good fit for each other? If so, it is time to move on to the structuring stage of creating your Loving FLR.

Structure Your Loving FLR

Now that you have determined that you are indeed a great fit to establish a Loving FLR, it is time to structure your own to meet your relationship's needs.

Step 1

Understand Your Mission – A Loving Female Led Relationship is a relationship that empowers women.

Why is empowering the woman in the relationship important? When a man can fully empower the woman he loves she becomes stronger in every way. His support allows her to carry out her best vision for the success of the relationship while providing him with the love, kindness and support he needs to feel satisfied by their love.

Step 2

Identify the Fundamental Priorities of your Loving FLR – The basic goal of every Loving Female Led Relationship is for the man to ensure that the woman he loves feels safe, secure and cared for. The actions he needs to take to ensure that she has the full experience of his support are the **Fundamental Priorities** of their Loving FLR.

To identify the **Fundamental Priorities** of your Loving FLR he should ask her directly to express what actions he can take to ensure that she feels safe, secure and cared for. He can specifically ask her - *What can I do to make sure you feel loved?* She should make a list of 5 actions he can take to ensure that she feels safe, secure, cared for and loved.

Examples: *Tell me you love me more often. Take me on dates regularly. Compliment me. Recognize when I make myself beautiful for you. Touch me and hold me. Spend time with me without distractions. Help me to build my business. Take the kids out to the park so I have time to myself once a week. Spend time alone with me.*

Once the **Fundamental Priorities** of your Loving FLR have been established these requests become his duties in the relationship. He does not try to convince her that her requests are not reasonable or important. He respects her requests and strives to deliver them to the best of his ability.

Step 3

Set the Vision for the Progress of Your Loving FLR – A couple establishing a Loving FLR is wise enough to recognize that where they begin is not where they will end up. Sit down together to discuss the following questions as a team.

- In 20 years, what do we want our life together to be like?

- What 3 steps can we take today to place ourselves on the trajectory to achieve our vision?
- Which habits do we have that could hinder us from achieving our vision?

Step 4

Establish the Path for Your Loving FLR – Once you have established your long-term vision for your relationship, identified specific action steps that you can take to reach that goal and discussed the current actions that may hold you back, it is then time to establish the path to reach the full potential of your Loving FLR. Your established path should include daily actions you can take to ensure that you reach your vision. Discuss these points as a team.

- What are three tasks we can do daily to enable us to reach our vision for the relationship? Who is responsible for each of the tasks?
- What are our five major household duties? Who has the best skill set and wisdom to take responsibility for them?
- What is his favorite love language; words of affirmation, quality time, physical touch, acts of service, or receiving gifts? Ask him to share three ways she can ensure that he feels loved.

Step 5

Identify Roadblocks for Your Loving FLR – No relationship can be stable without a conversation about actions that could derail the progress of the relationship. Discuss these points openly as a team.

- What can he do to break her trust?
- What can she do to break his trust?
- What are his habits/traits that could potentially damage the relationship?
- What are her habits/traits that could potentially damage the relationship?
- Are there any unexpressed desires that she has for the relationship?
- Are there any unexpressed desires that he has for the relationship?

Create a list for each item identifying actions you can take to work together to reduce/eliminate the issue. Discuss all unexpressed desires to determine how to include them in your relationship without violating your personal values.

Step 6

Establish Success Points – Maintaining the peace and progress of your Loving Female Led Relationship takes a considerable amount of effort. This effort should be rewarded by establishing Success Points, dedicated markers to celebrate your success in maintaining the relationship.

Your Success Points should follow the 2/2/2 Method. Every two weeks you go out on a date to celebrate the success of your Loving FLR. Every 2 months you spend an entire weekend away (or a staycation) celebrating the success of your Loving FLR. Every 2 years you take the time to renew your vows celebrating the success of your Loving FLR.

Strengthen Your Loving FLR

The best way to strengthen your relationship is to create a goal and work towards it together, demonstrating that you are a team. Teamwork is the primary foundation for a successful Loving FLR.

When you can work towards a goal together, overcome obstacles together and stay the course and remaining faithful to your mission, you have overstepped one of the biggest hindrances to a relationship's success.

Start a small business together, set a fitness goal or commit to a lifestyle upgrade. Becoming a team working towards a common goal will help you to learn how to compromise, create solutions to issues and to remain faithful.

Enjoy a Long Distance Loving FLR

A Loving FLR is a relationship that empowers women and it can be enjoyed across the miles. In this digital age, long distance love is normal. A Long Distance Loving FLR is basically the same as having a local relationship, you just have to be more creative. A couple can enjoy a Long Distance Loving FLR by following these suggestions.

- When your partner shares a personal goal, create a way to become involved in it.
- Use a variety of social media platforms to surprise your partner with love notes.
- Plan outside date nights with your partner where you go out and stream live.
- Use social media to become the primary promoter of your partner's creativity and businesses.
- Have new experiences and enjoy activities offline so that you have you have interesting things to share with your partner.
- Send old-fashioned love letters in the mail to each other.
- Create an online social group (or join one) that interacts regularly so that you have the same social circle.

Spice Up Your Loving FLR

Life can become routine for any couple, idly moving alone, maintaining life. Thankfully, those in a Loving FLR are open minded enough to embrace these thrilling experiences.

Explore Deeper Sexual Intimacy

A couple in a Loving FLR should explore deepening their sexual intimacy together. There are secret sexual desires hidden within each of us, causing us to feel mentally repressed because we cannot express the truth of what gives us the most thrilling pleasure.

Discovering and engaging in sexual play that provokes an immediate sexual arousal will create a deeper intimacy that the act of serving and supporting each other cannot touch. What turns you on sexually that you don't believe anyone will understand because you don't understand it yourself? Sharing this sexual play time with your partner will create a bond that is unmatched by any other relationship. *Ooh! You can diddle me like I really like it? Yes, I'll love you forever!*

In order to explore and achieve deeper sexual intimacy, a couple in a Loving FLR can start by finding a website that offers erotic stories. Take the time to browse the stories individually and choose one that excites you. Email the link to the story to your partner so that they can read it. Do this once per week until the stories you choose begin to reveal your secret fantasies. Discuss these secret fantasies with your partner.

Even if you choose not to engage in this fantasy in real life, revealing this type of secret to your partner and having them honor, accept and engage in it with you will be the absolute best factor in cementing your commitment to each other.

Challenge Him

The man who really enjoys supporting his partner in a Loving FLR is the type of man who will enjoy being challenged to do more and become more. Have fun with this type of man by asking for things that will keep him on his toes. Creating fun challenges for him will keep his mind centered around you in a good way. His mundane life will suddenly be sent into overdrive because he will never know what to expect from one of your requests.

You could ask him to prepare dinner but to make it more interesting give him a specific recipe to follow that includes 3 courses. Here are a few other suggestions for creating fun challenges your partner will enjoy.

- Ask him to call you specifically at 9:27 am to see how your morning is going.
- Ask him to select his work clothes for the week and submit each outfit for your approval.
- Ask him to do something he does not enjoy doing, like going shopping with you, and ask him to smile the entire time.
- Ask him to get your name tattooed on his booty.
- Ask him to grow a beard.
- Ask him to learn how to style your hair for you.
- Ask him to take you on two vacations this year instead of one.
- Ask him to earn another degree or license.
- Ask him to write you a love poem and stand in front of you and read it to you.
- Ask him to learn a choreographed dance routine with you so that you can perform it together at the next family gathering.

Plan a Monthly Spice Night

Since he is completely devoted to giving the woman he loves what she wants, any way she wants it, it is time for her to shine and deliver.

For one night a month, tantalize him with his greatest secrets, arouse him with his fantasies and immerse him in his fears. When a person focuses on their fears consistently, their fears and fantasies are often the same thing, which can reveal the secret desires of the heart.

Give him the date of your Spice Night in advance so that he will look forward to it but do not tell him what to expect. Blind fold him as you invite him to your Spice Night event specifically designed to thrill his heart and pull him closer to yours.

Celebrate Your Loving FLR

March 21st is established as **Loving FLR Day.** On this day, from sunrise to sunset, show appreciation for the Powerful Women in your lives through words and deed. Celebrate by wearing variations of BOLD GOLD colors and accessories to demonstrate your support of Loving FLRs.

Official Song of Loving Female Led Relationships

 Shining Star by **The Manhattans**

CHAPTER 5

Loving FLR Stories

These are true stories of Loving Female Led Relationships that have been edited for clarity and privacy.

Terri's Loving FLR

I wasn't really hoping for much of anything when I met Preston. After being divorced and single for 5 years I truly thought that men were only capable of being a pass-time and not taken seriously. I didn't give anyone a chance to love me because I thought it would be a waste of time.

I met Preston at a community event; it was a gathering of neighbors trying to improve our area. I saw that he was assisting one of the female leaders very gently and kindly, almost as though he enjoyed attending to her needs. I was impressed and when I saw him alone I introduced myself. He told me that he owned a house down the street and that I was welcome to come by anytime. I thought he was flirting and since he was attractive, I took him up on his offer.

One evening led to 5 in a row and we were almost obsessed with each other. I only took breaks to go to my apartment to change clothes and I would head right back to his place to spend more time with him. He was so interesting to me and I loved the way he would attend to my needs, just like he did with the woman he was helping at the community event. I was hooked! I wanted more and more and he always smiled when I told him that I appreciated him.

I wouldn't allow our time together to stand in the way of his work and I would leave for a little while he was asleep so that he wouldn't protest. After about four months of us enjoying our time together he asked me how I felt about him and I told him that I really cared about him. I remember that he smirked and asked, "You care?" as though I was trying to hide my real feelings. I just shrugged it off and went back to cuddling with him.

The strangest thing happened over the next few months. Preston seemed to be fueled by my appreciation for how he cared for me. The more I told him that he was amazing, the more amazing things he did for me. He cooked for me. He cleaned up after me. He even started my car on cold mornings so it would be warm for me when I got in to drive. He made great love to me anytime I even hinted that I needed it.

Soon he was involving himself in every aspect of my life. We began to depend on each other and divide up our life duties. He would bring the food and I would cook. We shared a phone account. He added me to his roadside assistance program. We began paying on installments for a vacation together. He added me as an authorized user on his credit card. I began assisting his sister with baby-sitting her children. He joined my cousins on their fantasy football league. Even though we didn't explicitly say it, we were joining our lives together which showed me that he wanted me to be a part of his future.

We became so entangled that if we had split up it would take some major overhauling to not have to contact each other. But I was glad because I didn't want to split up with him. I enjoyed him. I felt safe with him and for the first time in my life I felt like I was a priority in someone's life.

A year after meeting him he asked me to move in with him and I did without hesitation. I wanted more of him every single day and he gave without ever acting as though the things I wanted were too much. I will admit that I can be pessimistic at times but his concern for me helped me to stop thinking the entire world was trying to reject me.

With his support I ended up getting my real estate license and flourishing in my career. I went from renting an apartment to owning homes of my own. I lost weight. I stopped smoking. I didn't change myself *for* him; I changed myself *because* of him. His love and support allowed me to be a better woman even though he never demanded that I change anything.

If I could give advice to women who have lost hope in love I would like to say, it's real. I never thought someone would come along to love me in my broken pieces and inspire me to heal myself. He was patient as I learned to accept his love as real and he was kind enough to forgive me when I wasn't being patient with myself. I do not boss him around or force him to do what I want him to do. I take care of the maintenance of our household when I have time to do so and we make all of our major decisions together. Our relationship is a Loving FLR because he places my happiness as his priority and he enjoys doing it so much that it really does feel like a reward for not giving up on love.

Phoenix's Loving FLR

I had a huge crush on Demetrius the first time I saw him. He was wearing dark blue jeans and a white shirt. He was in good shape with curly blond hair, pale skin, deep green eyes that were ready to smile and joke, but one could see that there was depth to them, like the eyes of somebody who has seen too much too soon. He was so smart and driven.

But I knew my crush was hopeless. He was much younger than me and I was the owner and CEO of the company that had just hired him. I was in my late 40s and overweight - men did not notice me as a woman. He did not notice me as a woman either, which was just as well, as anything else would have been weird and inappropriate.

That was a time of my life of bitterness and frustration and some anger. My previous relationships had all failed early on. I was trying to resign myself to staying single. As I said, men did not notice me as a woman anymore, and that was painful. I was unhappy about my desperate crush and maybe hated myself a bit for it. I suppose the combination of those factors made me behave in a certain way that gave Demetrius the impression that I really did not like him as a colleague, which was not true.

He was working closely with a good friend of mine and they became good friends. I had confided my crush to her and one day she decided to speak to him about my feelings behind my back because she did not want him to mistake my curt behavior for general rudeness. Apparently, he was confused and surprised by this knowledge. He wrote me a long email in which he apologized for never seeing my feelings, for being defensive around me, for coming across as superficial. He wrote that he wanted to improve and fix things between us. We exchanged emails, then talked, and eventually decided to have a date.

A weird thing I realized then is that because of our age difference, because of my position, because of my previous failed relationships, because of my bitterness and anger, and maybe also because of how painful my crush had been so far, I did not at all imagine a symmetrical relationship with him as something I could get into. The words "girlfriend" and "boyfriend" didn't sound to me like something we could ever be.

I don't think those words sounded any better to him. I don't think he was imagining a relationship with me. He wanted to diffuse the tension between us and was a bit curious.

On our first date we ended up making some jokes about house husbands and how they should be taking care of housework or something like that. He thought the concept was interesting. We continued dating for a while until I said that that had to stop because I was afraid that all this would end poorly and I would just get hurt again. He said that he was serious and willing to prove it. This is how I ended up setting some conditions and expectations for our relationship, and I was surprised that he was able to keep up with them.

Over the following weeks and months my expectations for his part of our relationship ended up progressing further and deeper. I was surprised how bossy I could be, and I was surprised he would play along with it. Our lives got so mutually entangled, we soon recognized that we were too deep into this to ever emerge.

Several times I had concerns about his well-being. I wondered if this relationship was really good for him and I worried that I would lose him. Every time I expressed my fears, he took it upon himself to work hard to prove that he would not break my heart and every time his diligence brought us deeper into Loving FLR territory.

Fast forward 5 years and now we have a well-established Loving FLR. Things have really progressed a lot. I handle the finances, ensuring that this is very far from a dating-the-CEO-for-her-money sort of situation, and he handles the housework. He is subject to a number of restrictions and rules. His focus is making me happy and as the woman who is usually in charge, I need that.

That is my first relationship to last more than a few months. By believing it impossible, I was not trying to disguise myself, I was feeling free to be myself and unafraid of consequences. Demetrius also never expected this to last nor to find himself in the position in which he is now. He was taking it a step at a time with curiosity and a bit of bewilderment until one day he found himself in love with the woman ruling his world. He loves the challenge of pushing himself for me and he believes that my guidance helps him improve.

Kevin's Loving FLR

I am Kevin and with me is my wife, Sarah. I am an immigrant from Germany DE and living with my wife in Los Angeles. I am 27 and she is 30. I am the owner of a coffee bar in Sunset Boulevard and a PhD student whereas my wife has her own business in Construction.

I met Sarah during my broke days in UCLA Berkeley when I was desperately looking for a job. I dreamed and still plan to build up my career in Diplomacy and Foreign Affairs. My wife was a strong independent woman but unfortunately a heartbroken single mom when I first met her. I suffered 5 rejections and 3 heartbreaks before meeting Sarah. She had only one heartbreak during her final year at UCLA.

It was not love at first sight. Our relationship was about helping each other with favors. My wife wanted to help me with a job while I wanted to help her with raising our daughter (although I am not the father). She asked me to marry her only when I got so close to our daughter that she called me "Dad" during the 4th year of our relationship.

As the proverb says "Happy Wife Happy Life" so I have always tried my best to make sure she feels better than before. It takes a lot of effort but yes, I got accustomed eventually. Our relationship is different from others in a way that my wife is financially independent and powerful. In our marriage both me and Sarah work yet Sarah earns more than I do. It is kind of hard sometimes to get along with an strong willed woman but yes, the effort really pays off. There is nothing more beautiful in this world than the love of a strong woman.

Both me and Sarah love traveling and we are health geeks so we start our day by running a distance of almost 5 miles before the sun rises every morning. To keep our relationship exciting we resort to simple stuff like pillow fights, painting, working with cardboard boxes to make toys and a lot more. Our excitement is doubled thanks to Doreen (our pet Alsatian). And so far, we have travelled to Sweden, Finland, Spain, Switzerland, Bulgaria, Slovakia, Ukraine, Estonia and Turkey. We travel around Europe every winter with the exception that 2020 failed us.

It was Sarah who inspired me to be a health geek, not because I was overweight but rather because I hardly ate or slept properly. I decided to stop working as a Barista and purchase the coffee bar I worked for because Sarah suggested that I earn more money for our daughter Maria's school classes and admission. Apart from that I decided to take a PhD degree in International Relations because Sarah suggested it, although I was reluctant. I decided to listen to her because she says that a higher level of study will help me make a name for myself. She also helped me understand that a higher qualification will help me earn respect from my future seniors at the Department of The State.

In a Loving FLR I came to understand that a woman loves her companion truly because she knows how to love herself. I love her because I was under the influence of my mother who has always avoided the romantic and masochistic games that our culture has always forced us to do. My relationship has gained me enough criticism; my friends have always tried to convince me that my marriage is doomed to fail because I follow her lead. But as time passed by, I discovered that Sarah is incapable of abusing me. As a token of appreciation, I prefer to stay back home and do the traditional stuff that women in a misogynist society do. I am not forced to do it; I do because I want to. My life without our Loving FLR would eventually end up as a temporary relationship where I would forever feel self-guilt for being too obsessed with my own needs.

The best way to support a woman is to stand by her during her tough times no matter how strong she is. Even though some women are strong, they do not have a frozen heart. They know how to love too, and they love the hardest. Supporting a strong woman is about paying attention to her needs and doing what is needed to keep her calm.

Nia's Loving FLR

I remember quite clearly the day our relationship took an unexpected turn. Alex and I had been together for 2 years and living together for a year already. We were deeply committed to each other but we were always fighting. I was beginning to think that we had made a mistake and that our love wasn't real. One night I remember crying because I felt like he didn't get me. He turned to me, obviously annoyed and asked me, "What do you need from me?"

I cried harder because - *I didn't know*. He walked out of the room and I fell asleep crying. The next day I woke up and he was awake sitting beside me. I sat up and looked over at him and he pulled me closer to him, hugged me and asked, "What can I do to make you happy?" I shrugged and told him that I would think about it and let him know later. We kissed and went on about our day. He went to work and so did I.

While at work I was thinking about the question that he asked me. I decided to make a list of things he could do to make me happy.

My list was: *Take me out on dates twice a month, hug me whenever you come home from work, tell me I'm beautiful, wear the gifts I bought for you, cook for ME sometimes, watch the movies I want to watch sometimes, ask me about my day sometimes*

I sat there looking over my list wondering how he would react. I sent the list to him in an email and told him that we could talk about it later. Later that evening we sat down to have dinner together and I asked if he had gotten my email. He put his fork down, stood up and walked over to stand behind me. He hugged me tightly and kissed me on the top of my head and said, *"I'm sorry I wasn't doing those things for you. I'll do better."*

After that night, things surely improved. I would catch him reading a printed version of my list that he kept in his nightstand. He didn't do everything right away, but one at a time I saw him taking note to do the things that made me feel cared for. I was so happy that he was concerned with my needs and was eager to fulfill them. I became excited to see him. I felt loved and appreciated just because he was making an effort and I returned the effort by doing more for him.

I stopped nagging and allowed him to be good to me. He was so happy that I was more relaxed around him. The fights we always had slowed down because I finally felt like my feelings mattered. I see now that I should have expressed my needs directly instead of hoping he would guess what they were; that made all the difference. He wasn't ignoring my needs, he just didn't know what they were.

William's Loving FLR

I couldn't catch up to her in time. I would see her often at business mixers, flittering around the room, talking to people, handing out business cards, smiling and laughing. I wanted to meet her because I thought she was beautiful and obviously everyone loved her but by the time I was able to get close to her, she was always on her way out of the door-- with another man.

I would go to every professional mixer in the city hoping to run into her and I finally found out her name -Kristen- and looked her up. I learned that she was a public relations professional and an author. She owned her own firm. I was impressed. I saw on her company's website that they were hosting a children's fall festival and I decided to volunteer just so I could meet her.

She wasn't at the volunteer training but I had my hopes up that I would be able to talk to her at the actual event. When I saw her there, clipboard in one hand, a water bottle in the other, I walked up to her and she smiled at me. I introduced myself, she introduced herself and thanked me for volunteering. Then she walked away without another word.

I got up the courage to call her but when I did her assistant told me that she doesn't take calls and that I would have to set up a meeting, so I did. When I walked into her office I could smell a sweet vanilla fragrance as she rose to shake my hand. I sat down in front of her desk and smiled at her.

"What brings you in today?" she asked me, much like a medical doctor.

"I..I wanted to meet you," I stammered.

"Ok," she said and raised an eyebrow. "We've met. Now what?"

"I would like to take you out on a date," I spoke confidently and then immediately dropped the pen I was holding.

"Why?" she asked, seeming to enjoy my discomfort.

"Why? Uh. Because I would like to get to know you better," I said cautiously.

"What are you offering?" she asked.

"Dinner? I guess. Or lunch."

"I have people to get those taken care of for me. Why would I need you?"

I almost choked. It was the way she said it that got me, daring me to continue.

"Well, I want to spend time with you," I reasoned.

"You want. You want. Why should I care what you want?" she challenged me firmly, yet sweetly.

I didn't have an answer for that.

"Well," she said slowly. "Why don't you come back when you have an answer for me?" She stood up to shake my hand again.

I rose as well and looked into her eyes. "I want what you want," I told her.

She cocked her head to the side as though she was considering what I had just said.

"I want what you want. If you tell me what you want, I'll want the same," I told her earnestly.

"Hmm. I want you to be back here at 8 tonight with a box of thin mint Girl Scout cookies, a blue lighter and a friendship bracelet."

Huh?

"Can you do that?" she asked and bit her lip, stifling a smile.

"I can do that," I replied.

"See you at 8," she said and laughed. It was the first time I heard her laugh and it was just the motivation I needed to get my errands done.

I met her that evening with everything that she asked for and she laughed so hard that she had to hold herself steady by gripping her desk. This broke the ice between us and we sat in her office and at thin mints while talking and listening to music for nearly three hours.

We did have some things in common like our work ethic and drive for excellence but our experiences growing up and our views on life's mysteries were completely different. It intrigued me that she was not at all religious and she was surprised that I was raised on a farm. Our differences only made us want to know more about each other and over time it gave us lots to discuss. I kept my promise when I told her that I wanted what she wanted. It wasn't difficult to follow her lead because she wasn't aggressive or hurtful. Kristen didn't need to use me for her benefit because her life was already great.

I loved that she was kind and sincere and she was used to having things done her way. I wanted to give her more of that because she was actually very easy to please and I enjoyed pleasing her. I loved making her smile and laugh. I enjoyed the look on her face when I took care of a small task that she had forgotten or she was too tired to do. I can't help her with her business but the little things I could do, I did. She was always so grateful. She would acknowledge my small favors with a few small favors of her own that left me speechless. I felt like a real man when I was around Kristen because she didn't need me but I knew I added something special that she couldn't hire anyone to do.

Two years after we met, I proposed marriage to her. She accepted the ring but told me that she would rather not get legally married. I accepted her decision but I still treat her as though she is my wife and she treats me as though I am her husband. We have a good life together; she's always planning offbeat trips or sending me off on crazy challenges that make her laugh. I love that laugh so much that whatever is on the list she gives me, I am happy to bring back to her.

Stephanie's Loving FLR

The big thing that men need to realize about supporting their wife/girlfriend is it comes back to them. They'll usually get more support because they are giving it. The household is going to be more at peace. Communication is going to be better as they both can know that the other will listen. If he doesn't support his wife, she is going to withdraw, possibly go into depression, and be less willing to support or talk with him as a mechanism to try to protect herself. And this goes both ways.

As someone who does have a partner who supports me in every way, I feel very happy, fulfilled, and loved! Coming from a not-so-great background, having a partner like this was confusing at first but after understanding that this person really cares about me and what I want to do, it was easy to let go of that feeling of having to be perfect or the feeling of not being good enough or smart enough to do the things I wanted to do.

I get to be excited about my days and even if I fail, I know he'll be right there to pick me up so fear of failure isn't so scary anymore.

Things he does to make me feel this way and support me:

- Understanding when I work later than him, he'll take over dinner
- Actively listens about my day and only offers advice when asked
- Encourages me to keep going even if I feel like I didn't do well that day, saying "tomorrow is a new day"
- Telling me I'm awesome when I talk about my accomplishments

There are so many other things but these are the main reasons why I flourish because of his support.

Maya's Loving FLR

My husband basically had a firm belief that he was going to spend the rest of his life alone at 18 because he thought nobody could love him. He grew up being bullied for no reason. He had anxiety problems and he couldn't even go to store or pay for his stuff by himself, as his mom told me.

We met online through an art chat group. I lived in Indonesia and he was in the US. We connected and dated (it was me who asked him out). This 18-year-old boy with massive social anxiety traveled alone to Indonesia to meet me eight months later. His parents couldn't even believe it.

I still don't know what I did specifically to inspire him to put in all of that effort but he felt loved and he told me he's been using me as an emotional crutch ever since. Slowly, I got him to open up to me. I let him know that sharing his feelings to me is safe and that I will not betray him like his friends turned enemies. I assured him that I am a trustworthy ally to him.

I'm a happy go lucky type of a person. I am outgoing, brave, about 60% extroverted, and by nature I'm a positive person, when I'm not depressed. Because of this I was a positive influence to him in many ways. We dated long distance for four years before we got married and he traveled to Indonesia to see me each and every summer break he had in college. This year will be our 11th wedding anniversary.

When you care about someone, you don't have to be asked to do something for them; you're just willing as long it's within your limitations, of course.

It was a lot of work behind the scenes but we rarely fight and when we did have a disagreement it was never bad. We've had no physical altercations, we've had no flying China, we don't scream at the top of our lungs. The key is good communication. Open up and tell me what you want or need from me. We're also actively trying to be the best versions of ourselves without losing our identities but cut off/ reduce the annoying habits as well as we could.

We're not perfect but we know how to laugh. We constantly make fun of each other in a friendly manner, not with ill intentions. My husband was so closed off before, now he over shares things with me. We are best friends.

It's not going to be easy at first but try to explain your thought process to see if he understands it.

That's one way to identify a problem. It's always a good thing to become self-aware. We like to discuss things like this over dinner or just any time when the topic comes up, really. What made me act like this? How did I become this person?

Psychology wasn't something I thought of before but I became more interested in it because of him and now I'm quite invested. I was pretty selfish and lacked empathy before. He's an empath so he taught me things, directly and indirectly. I have to say he made me a better person too.

CHAPTER 6

Frequently Asked Questions

Q: Is a Loving FLR a gender role reversal in a relationship? Is the man required to take on household chores and be a stay-at-home husband?

A: No. A Loving FLR is a relationship that empowers and honors the choices of women. It is designed so that women can feel seen and heard by their partners. There is no set way to structure your Loving FLR because each woman's needs and desires are different. While one woman may enjoy running a business, another woman may enjoy catering to her husband's needs. The key factor in a Loving FLR is to listen to what will satisfy the woman and do your best to give that to her.

Q: Is the man in a Loving FLR obligated to say Yes at all times?

A: Absolutely not. The man in a Loving FLR wants to say Yes as often as he can because he enjoys caring for the woman he loves. He never feels obligated to say Yes because he understands that his participation in a Loving FLR is his choice and a representation of his skills. Many men cannot say Yes to the requests of the woman that they love because they lack the capability to do so. A man who can say Yes to most of the requests of his loving partner is wise and has developed a skillset that is so impressive that he seems to be able to provide anything that she could ever want. How many men can say that?

Q: How is a Loving FLR different from a male led relationship, other than the gender of the leader?
A: The difference is, its purpose. A Loving FLR balances the destruction of our patriarchal society and allows women to finally be seen and heard so that they can contribute more to the advancement of our society.

Q: When the woman leads the relationship is it like a dictatorship?
A: No. When the Grand Marshall leads a parade is he a dictator? He simply paves the way by being grand and setting the pace for the parade. The parade members follow by choice. A woman's leadership is the same. She sets the vision for the relationship and her partner chooses to follow her lead.

Q: When the Loving FLR is skewed to the woman's advantage what mechanism are there to prevent neglect and abuse?
A: There is no obligation in a Loving FLR. The man has the freedom to pull back his support if he does not feel respected or cared for. The man is responsible for choosing to give the gift of a Loving FLR to a woman he trusts will not abuse it. If he chooses the wrong woman, it is his liability.

Q: What does the woman in a FLR give back to the relationship?

A: A woman in a Loving FLR feels safe, secure and cared for. Therefore, she can offer the same sentiments back to her partner. When a woman is not being loved properly she cannot contribute the best of herself to the well-being of her family or her husband. When a woman is being cared for and properly supported by her husband, she is then able to attend to his needs without hesitation. If he is ensuring that she is happy, she will turn back and give the same to him.

Q: From what I've learnt about Loving FLRs the woman molds the man to her liking, even choses his friends sometimes. After her tinkering, for lack of a better word, is he the man she fell in love with, or is he an accessory? I mean he's been stripped of his individually in the name of improvement.

A: The scenario you described is not indicative of a Loving FLR. You must have misread or misinterpreted my teachings or you may have been tricked by a man's interpretation. There are many websites that teach about Female Led Relationships but those are websites written by men who are trying to convince women to abuse them by taking away their rights and privileges. Many men crave abuse, dominance and control as a sexual trigger. They call it a Female Led Relationship because they want to be led around like animals. A **Loving FLR** will not satisfy them because this relationship style is based on mutual respect, love and concern for the relationship's progress. A Loving FLR is in no way based on control.

The woman in a Loving FLR does not mold the man to her liking. She may offer him suggestions for his personal improvement for things that she sees that are hindering his progress like drug or alcohol abuse, poor hygiene or a sloppy work ethic. He maintains his individuality. He wants to be the best he can be for the woman he loves so he does not ignore her suggestions for improvement because he trusts her judgment.

Q: Why would a man admit that he is involved in a Loving FLR? Wouldn't this bring shame to him as a man?
A: Honestly, men who are involved in Loving FLRs do not feel shame about their relationships because they are experiencing a relationship that satisfies their soul. These men are happier than they have ever been and they wouldn't trade this experience for the approval of friends, family or strangers.

Q: Is there a penchant of women in Loving FLRs to mildly humiliate their partners by putting them in awkward situations?
A: A woman who respects the man she loves would never want to humiliate him to demonstrate her power. A woman in a Loving FLR is a protector of the man who has devoted himself to supporting her.

Q: If you were to encounter a Loving FLR in reverse, what are the chances you'd condemn the man as a self-absorbed and controlling?

A: A Loving FLR in reverse is still a Loving FLR simply because the woman gives back to the man what he gives to her.

Q: What is the difference between matriarchy and patriarchy? What makes one (matriarchy) right and the other (patriarchy) wrong?
A: Patriarchy has demonstrated that it is devastating to our society's progress. Matriarchy has yet to be upheld and tested to see its effects. A Loving FLR is not rooted in the concept of Matriarchy at all. It actively upholds the principle that the woman's voice, opinions and desires are equally as important as any man's.

Q: When a lady asks me what I am looking for, how do you suggest I share that I seek a Loving FLR without overloading them?
A: Just say, I'm looking for an amazing woman to create a happy life with. You don't have to convince a woman to participate in a Loving FLR, all you have to do is give it to her.

Q: How do one meet a mature Dominant Female on internet? Most dominant Females seem to be young and maybe not truly dominant.
A: If you are seeking a woman to dominate you, you should pay one to do so. Aggressive Dominance has no in a Loving FLR.

Q: Many women tell me that they want a guy who is more dominant with them. Can a women really love a man if he is not dominant?

A: All women are different and have different needs. A woman who expresses that she wants a man who is dominant or will take control of situations and her is merely expressing what she wants from her relationship. When a woman expresses what she wants in her relationship and the man provides it for her, he is ensuring her happiness, which is still a Loving FLR.

Q: Is a man in a Loving FLR considered to be weak?

A: A man who is capable of providing a woman the support she needs to flourish cannot be considered weak unless the woman believes that she should be subjugated and she craves abuse.

Q: Does the woman give rules to a man in a Loving FLR?

A: All women express their needs in a relationship differently. Some women may like to feel as though they are in control by offering a man rules. Other women would say they are offering suggestions to a man when she feels he needs correction. A man who enjoys having rules and being controlled will only be attracted to a woman who can offer this type of communication style. A man who enjoys a softer type of love and mature communication would not be a part of a relationship where he feels like a woman rules over him.

Q: What about children who witness a Loving FLR, how will they be affected?

A: Children who witness a happy mother and a devoted father will likely model that behavior and have the same expectations for their own relationships. A Loving FLR has no aggression, abuse or controlling behavior which is exactly what we want our children to witness and imitate in their own relationships.

CHAPTER 7

Study Guide

Chapter 1 Review
Does a Woman Need a Man?

1) Why would a woman believe she doesn't need a man?
2) A Loving Female Led Relationship is described as what type of relationship?
3) In a Loving FLR what is the man's primary focus?
4) What can being supported by a man in a Loving FLR teach a woman?
5) How does this patriarchal society hurt men?
6) If men are not automatic leaders and women are not automatic leaders, then who should take the lead?
7) When a woman feels safe, secure and cared for, how does she relate to the man who loves her?
8) If a Loving FLR is not about the woman controlling the relationship, then what is it about?
9) What are 3 problems that a Loving FLR resolves?
10) How does a Loving FLR promote intimacy?
11) What are the gender role expectations in a Loving FLR?

Chapter 2 Review
The Woman's Role in a Loving FLR

1) What happens when a woman does not believe she can have the type of relationship she really wants?
2) How does being an intentional leader impact the relationship?
3) What are 3 ways a woman can prepare for a Loving FLR?
4) Why should a woman create a life she loves before she meets the man who will love her?
5) What is the key ingredient to creating a Loving FLR?
6) When men enjoy women who demand or control them, what can you tell about their past experiences with women?
7) Why is it important to allow a man time to learn how to love you?
8) What does it mean to be a man's safe space?
9) What is Affirmative Correction and how do you do it?
10) What should a woman do instead of reducing a man's ego?

Chapter 3 Review
The Man's Benefit in a Loving FLR

1) How do you recognize a Gentleman?
2) What power does a man have in a Loving FLR?
3) What inspires some men to behave aggressively towards women?
4) How does a man demonstrate his strength in a Loving FLR?
5) Which trait do men often have to hide in average relationships?
6) How can a man motivate a woman to become a Boss personality?
7) How can a man demonstrate the agrees with a woman's dreams?
8) When should a man say No to a woman's request?
9) What 3 things can you do to promote peace in your relationship?
10) When should a man put a woman in her place?
11) How does a man promote the woman he loves?
12) How does a man protect the woman he loves?

Chapter 4 Review
How to Create a Loving FLR

1) What is the first way to recognize a good potential partner?
2) Why is respecting your partner's judgment important in a Loving FLR?
3) Who is the ultimate winner in a Loving FLR?
4) How do you know if you and your partner are good for each other?
5) What are two ways to identify if you and your partner are a good fit for each other?
6) What is the overall mission of a Loving FLR?
7) How do you establish the Fundamental Priorities in a Loving FLR?
8) Thinking about your life together in 20 years is an example of doing what for your Loving FLR?
9) What is the primary foundation for a Loving FLR?
10) What are 3 ways to add spice to your Loving FLR?

A NOTE FROM THE AUTHOR

Dear Reader,

Thank you for taking the time to read this book to learn more about how to create a Loving Female Led Relationships. You have gotten to know me quite well as I have dished out my best wisdom for creating a mature, healthy relationship that will help improve our society.

If you have benefitted from this book, please leave a review to let me know.

Thank you.

Te-Erika

Visit Us Online

LovingFLR.Com – Our blog for Loving Female Led Relationships

FLRStyle.Com – Our Online Boutique with FLR clothing, jewelry and classes.

FLRMatchMakingService.Com – We connect Powerful Women with Gentlemen who Adore Them

Made in the USA
Middletown, DE
11 March 2022